CLASSICAL FAVOURITES
Playalong *for* Violin

Wise Publications
part of The Music Sales Group
London/New York/Paris/Sydney/Copenhagen/Berlin/Madrid/Tokyo

Published by
Wise Publications
14/15 Berners Street, London W1T 3LJ, UK.

Exclusive Distributors:
Music Sales Limited
Distribution Centre, Newmarket Road, Bury St. Edmunds,
Suffolk IP33 3YB, UK.
Music Sales Corporation
180 Madison Avenue, 24th Floor, New York NY10016, USA
Music Sales Pty Limited
Units 3-4, 17 Willfox St, Condell Park, NSW, 2200 Australia

Order No. AM984489
ISBN 1-84609-310-4
This book © Copyright 2006 Wise Publications,
a division of Music Sales Limited.

Arranging and Engraving supplied by Camden Music.
Edited by Ann Farmer.
Cover photography by George Taylor.
Printed in Great Britain.

CDs recorded, mixed and mastered by Jonas Persson.
Instrumental solos by Robert Simmons.
Piano: Tau Wey

www.musicsales.com

A Musical Joke (Presto), K522

Composed by Wolfgang Amadeus Mozart

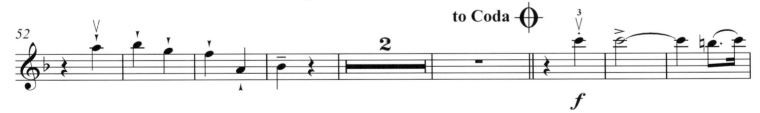

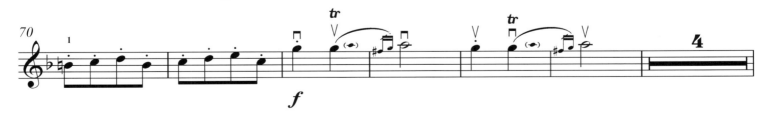

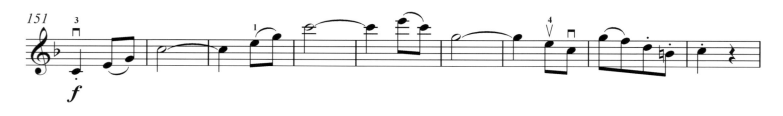

rit.

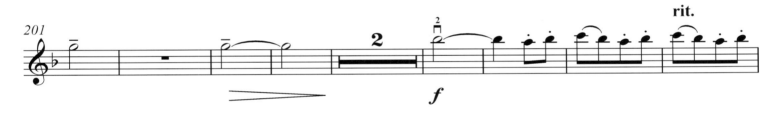

D.S. al Coda
(without repeats)

a tempo

Coda

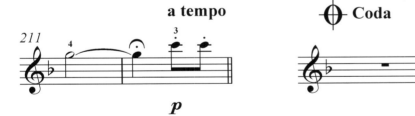

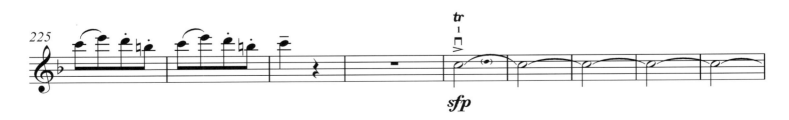

Air (from 'The Water Music')

Composed by George Frideric Handel

Moderato

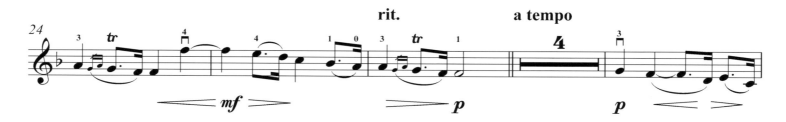

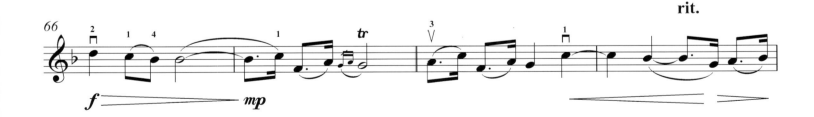

Allegretto Theme (from Symphony No.7)

Composed by Ludwig van Beethoven

Ave Maria

Composed by Franz Peter Schubert

Lento ($\downarrow$ = 72)

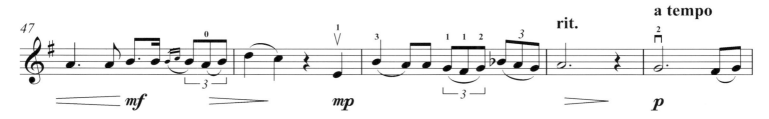

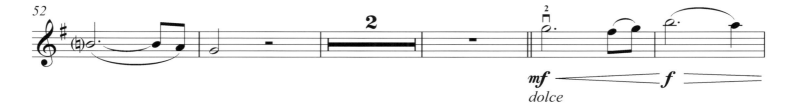

Entr'acte (from 'Rosamunde')

Composed by Franz Peter Schubert

Andantino (♩ = 72)

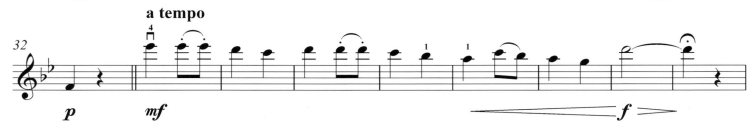

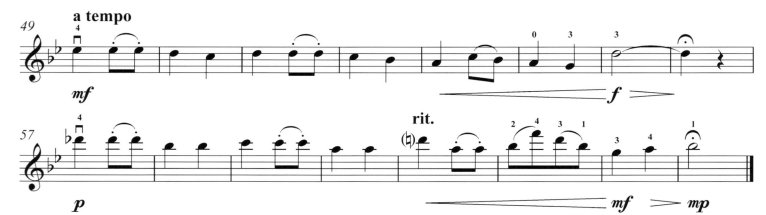

Jerusalem

Composed by Hubert Parry

Maestoso (♩ = 46)

Jesu, Joy Of Man's Desiring

Composed by Johann Sebastian Bach

Moderato ($\quad$ = 76)

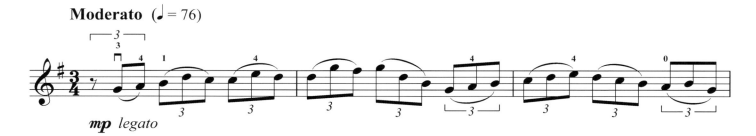

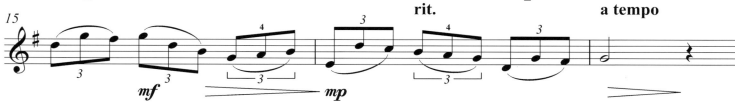

Largo (from 'Xerxes')

Composed by George Frideric Handel

Largo (♩ = 60)

rit.　　　　　　a tempo

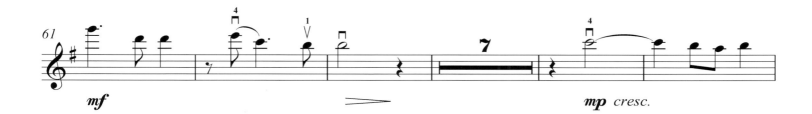

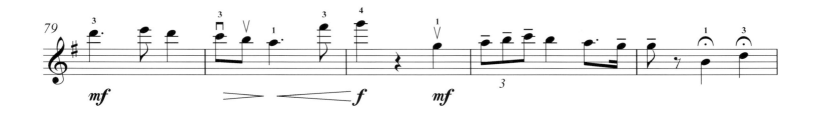

March (from 'The Nutcracker Suite')

Composed by Pyotr Ilyich Tchaikovsky

Tempo di marcia ($\quarternote$ = 144)

O For The Wings Of A Dove

Composed by Felix Mendelssohn

Con moto (♩ = 69)

a tempo

poco accel.

a tempo

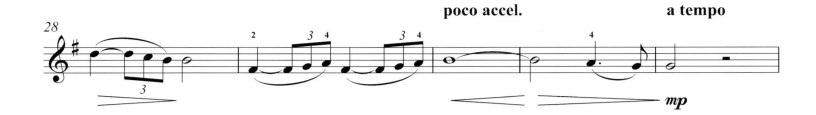

a tempo

rit.

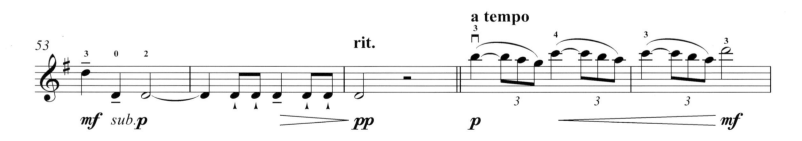

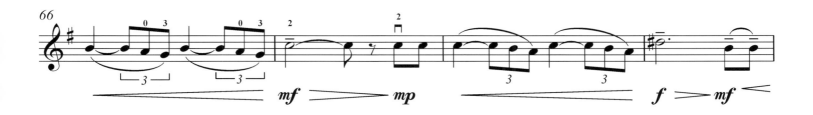

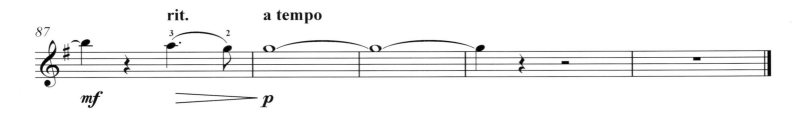

Sarabande (from Suite XI)

Composed by George Frideric Handel

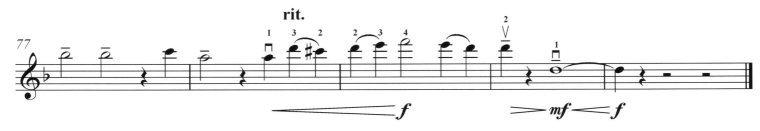

Bringing you the words and the music

All the latest music in print... rock & pop plus jazz, blues, country, classical and the best in West End show scores.

- Books to match your favourite CDs.

- Book-and-CD titles with high quality backing tracks for you to play along to. Now you can play guitar or piano with your favourite artist... or simply sing along!

- Audition songbooks with CD backing tracks for both male and female singers for all those with stars in their eyes.

- Can't read music? No problem, you can still play all the hits with our wide range of chord songbooks.

- Check out our range of instrumental tutorial titles, taking you from novice to expert in no time at all!

- Musical show scores include *The Phantom Of The Opera*, *Les Misérables*, *Mamma Mia* and many more hit productions.

- DVD master classes featuring the techniques of top artists.